MW00414655

# THE HOLY FACE

*"Behold, O God our protector: and look on the face of thy Christ. For better is one day in thy courts above thousands."*
—Psalm 83(84):10-11

O Jesus, Who in Thy cruel Passion didst become "the Reproach of men and the Man of Sorrows," I worship Thy Divine Face.

—St. Therese of the Child Jesus

# DEVOTION TO THE HOLY FACE

*"Convert us, O God: and show us
thy face, and we shall be saved."*
—Psalm 79(80):4

TAN Books
An Imprint of Saint Benedict Press, LLC
Charlotte, North Carolina

Nihil Obstat:    Philippus
                 Abbas Neo-Angelo Montanus

Imprimatur:    ✠ Carolus Hubertus
               Episcopus Sancti Josephi


Originally published at Clyde, Missouri. 3rd Edition, 1934; 83,000. Retypeset and republished by TAN Books, an Imprint of Saint Benedict Press, LLC, in 2010.

ISBN: 978-0-89555-903-6

Cover illustration: *St. Veronica* (oil on canvas), Reni, Guido (1575-1642), Pushkin Museum, Moscow, Russia/The Bridgeman Art Library International

Cover design: Sebrina Higdon

Printed and bound in the United States of America.


TAN Books
An Imprint of Saint Benedict Press, LLC
Charlotte, North Carolina
2012

ETERNAL Father, we offer Thee the Adorable Face of Thy Well-Beloved Son for the honor and glory of Thy Holy Name and for the salvation of all men.

—Blessed Pope Pius IX

# Contents

*Chapter 1*

# Merits Derived from Meditating On the Passion of Christ

THE devotion to the Passion of Our Lord and Saviour is, of all forms of Catholic devotion, the most ancient, the most venerable, the most universal. Jesus Himself has written the remembrance of His Passion deep into the hearts of His faithful. In order to imprint most deeply in our souls the remembrance of His Sacred Passion, Christ instituted Holy Mass, the unbloody renewal of the Sacrifice of the Cross.

For what reason did Jesus leave the impression of His bloody and disfigured Countenance on the cloth that Veronica presented to Him? Why did He take care to have the instruments of His Passion preserved, such as the Cross, the nails, the crown of thorns and the winding sheet? Was it not that we should keep vividly before us the remembrance of His bitter Passion?

1

Tauler, one of the great mystics of the Middle Ages, says: "Once when a venerable servant of God asked Our Lord what a man merited who exercised himself devoutly in meditating upon His Passion, Christ answered: 'By such meditation he merits:

1. To be cleansed from his sins.*
2. To have all his negligences supplied by the merits of My sufferings.
3. To be strengthened so that he will not easily be overcome by his enemies.
4. That My grace will be renewed in him as often as he reflects on My sufferings.
5. That I refuse him nothing that is profitable, if he earnestly ask for it.
6. That I lead him to perfection before his death.
7. That I assist him in his last hour, protect him against his enemies, and give him an assurance of salvation.'"

## Fruits of Meditation on the Passion

*It cleanses us from our sins.* It is impossible for a soul who takes Our Lord's

* Mortal sins, however, must be confessed.

sufferings seriously to heart, to continue offending God willfully, especially by mortal sin.

St. Alphonsus impresses this upon us by affirming: "A soul who believes in the Passion of Jesus Christ, and frequently thinks thereon, will find it impossible to go on offending her Saviour."

***It strengthens us against temptation.*** Frequent and devout meditation on the sufferings of Our Lord has the wonderful power to enable us to overcome our passions. St. Augustine writes in his *Confessions* that whenever he was tempted by the demon of impurity, he resisted Satan successfully by meditating on the Wounds of Jesus. "As often as I am tempted," he says, "I seek refuge in the Wounds of Jesus. I fly into the Heart of the mercies of my Lord!"

***It will lead us to perfection before our death.*** One of the principal sources of our sanctification is the tender and compassionate remembrance of our Saviour's sufferings. St. Bonaventure addresses these words to the soul seeking perfection: "If thou, O man, wouldst advance from virtue to virtue, if thou wouldst lead a perfect life, then meditate daily on the Passion of

Christ. Nothing else can so powerfully urge the soul to holiness. The painful Wounds of our Saviour's body penetrate even the hardest of hearts and inflame the coldest of souls with love."

*It gives us the assurance of a happy death.* St. Alphonsus Liguori says, "Souls that are tormented by the devil and tremble for their eternal salvation will feel great consolation in withdrawing their eyes from the outward world and fixing them on the Cross where Jesus hangs, bleeding from every wound."

*It insures for us a special glory in Heaven.* This was revealed to St. Gertrude. Once on the feast of St. John the Evangelist she beheld how this beloved Apostle enjoyed a special bliss in Heaven because he had always begun his contemplations with the remembrance of our Saviour's Passion, of which he had been an eye witness.

Moreover, we should love to meditate upon the Passion because therein our Saviour makes His virtues shine forth with great brilliance. He possesses every virtue in His soul, but the occasions of manifesting them especially arise in His Passion.

His immense love for His Father, His charity for mankind, hatred of sin, forgiveness of injuries, patience, meekness, fortitude, obedience to lawful authority, compassion— all these virtues shine forth in a heroic manner for our imitation. Jesus in His Passion is our Divine model in suffering. If, therefore, we frequently contemplate His sufferings and strive to imitate His virtues, we shall receive special graces which will transform us little by little into His likeness and prepare us to share in His glory in Heaven.

In reward for Veronica's sympathy,
Jesus impressed His Sacred Face upon her veil.

6

## Chapter 2

# The Imprint of Our Saviour's Blood-Stained Countenance on The Veil of Veronica

VENERATION of the dolorous Face of our Saviour Jesus Christ, as proved in Rome and practiced throughout the Church, had its beginning during the very Passion of Our Lord. It came to us through that heroic woman whose memory, from the first ages of Christianity, has been inseparably connected with the Sixth Station of the holy Way of the Cross and who is known to us as St. Veronica.*

The Son of God was being led forth to execution through the crowded streets of Jerusalem, followed by a shouting rabble which filled the air with loud, insulting cries. Our Divine Lord, exhausted by the

---

* The name *Veronica* means "true icon." According to Bl. Anne Catherine Emmerich, St. Veronica's actual name was *Seraphia.*—*Publisher,* 2010.

tortures of the night, fell beneath the heavy weight of His cross. A man, Simon of Cyrene, who was passing by, was compelled by the inhuman soldiers to assist Jesus in carrying the Cross. The sad procession had advanced but a short distance farther when suddenly a woman of majestic appearance broke through the infuriated mob *and offered our Saviour a veil as a sign of her compassion,* upon which He wiped His Adorable Face covered with sweat and blood. In reward for her sympathy, our Blessed Redeemer imprinted indelibly upon her veil the likeness of His Sacred Countenance.

## The Treasure of the Vatican

A tradition says that at the advice of St. Peter, Veronica later entrusted the holy Veil to the care of St. Clement, a noble Roman who was a disciple of St. Peter and his third successor in the See of Rome. From the hands of Pope St. Clement this venerated relic passed to his successors, who guarded it most carefully during the long years of persecution. Ever since that time the holy Veil has remained in Rome, where it is preserved with the greatest care as one of the most precious relics of the Vatican Basilica.

Every year in Lent the holy Veil is taken from the rich casket in which it is treasured, and from a high balcony erected around one of the pillars of the Vatican Basilica, it is exposed to the veneration of the faithful. An eye witness writes: "One cannot without feelings of tenderest compassion and sorrow look upon the noble brow covered with blood, the Divine eyes, livid and bloody, the whole Face pallid as in death. On the right cheek is seen the mark of the cruel blow inflicted by the brutal soldier, and on the left are traces of the insults of the Jews who spat upon Him. The nose is bruised and blood-stained, the mouth half open, the teeth broken, the beard disheveled and partly torn out, the hair matted with blood. But the whole Sacred Face, though disfigured, presents an appearance of *indescribable majesty and compassion, love and sadness.*"

The miraculous preservation of this Veil proves what great complacency Our Lord takes in the veneration of His Sacred Face.

# Transfiguration of the Holy Veil

In the memorable days of Pope Pius IX,* God deigned, by a touching prodigy, to glorify the Sacred Image venerated at the Vatican. It was during the exile of the Holy Father at Gaeta, in 1849, when the Veil of Veronica was allowed to be exposed for veneration from Christmas to Epiphany. On the third day of the exposition, the Veil, hitherto somewhat faded, became transfigured, as it were; the sacred features of our Saviour *appeared lifelike* and surrounded by a mild halo. Though covered with a piece of silk, which would normally prevent one from distinguishing them, the sacred features could, nevertheless, be distinctly seen. The Holy Face was of a deathly pallor, the eyes sunken, yet animated with an expression of profound sadness.

The canons who were guarding the Veil immediately notified their colleagues and the ecclesiastics of the Basilica. The bells were rung and the faithful flocked to the Vatican. The witnesses of this prodigy were filled with wonder and awe; many were in tears, all were visibly affected.

---

* Now *Blessed* Pope Pius IX.—*Publisher,* 2010.

## Chapter 3

## Chosen Souls Who Have Venerated the Thorn-Crowned Head of our Saviour

THROUGHOUT the centuries there have been chosen souls who have had special devotion to the Holy Face. Among the most illustrious were St. Augustine, St. Bernard, St. Gertrude the Great and St. Mechtilde. One of the most beautiful hymns in honor of the Sacred Face of Jesus* was composed by St. Bernard (d. 1153); another was written by St. Bonaventure (d. 1274). These saints worshiped in a special manner the thorn-crowned head of Christ.

The aim of the Church in propagating devotion to the Holy Face is *to impress ever more deeply on the minds of the faithful the memory of the sufferings of Our Lord,* that they may *nourish sorrow for their sins*

---

\* *"O Caput Cruentatum"*—"O Sacred Head." See English translation in Chapter 8.

and an ardent *desire to make reparation* for the offenses committed against the Divine Majesty.

## St. Gertrude

With wonderful clearness our Saviour impressed upon St. Gertrude how beneficial it is for a soul to meditate upon His sufferings and the great consolation He derives from the compassion thus offered Him. One day the Saint beheld Our Lord in the pitiable state in which He was bound to a pillar between two executioners, one of whom tore His flesh with thorns while the other lashed Him with scourges. Both of them struck Him on the Face, which was so disfigured that the sight of It filled Gertrude with bitter grief.

During the remainder of her life she could not restrain her tears whenever she remembered this sorrowful vision. It seemed to her as though Jesus turned His Face from side to side, but each time He did so, He was only struck the more cruelly by the other executioner. "Tell me, O Lord," exclaimed St. Gertrude, "*the remedy that can soothe the sufferings of Thy Divine Face.*" Jesus replied: "If anyone *meditates upon My sufferings* with tenderness and compassion, his heart will be to Me as a soothing balm for these wounds."

Frequently during her meditations St. Gertrude saw the Divine Countenance of our Saviour resplendent as the sun, illuminating priests, inflaming the devout and converting sinners. Once she asked why the blessed Countenance of our Redeemer shone like the sun, and she received this explanation: "Like the sun, *My Countenance illuminates, warms and fructifies.*"

On one occasion when St. Gertrude was compassionating the Adorable Face, wounded and disfigured, she asked Our Lord for a special grace for those who would practice this devotion. From His Divine lips she heard this consoling promise: "All those who meditate frequently on the vision of My Divine Face, attracted by the desires of love, shall receive within them, through My Humanity, a bright ray of My Divinity, which shall enlighten their inmost souls so that they shall reflect the light of My Countenance in a special manner throughout eternity."

## St. Mechtilde

Overcome with ardor, St. Mechtilde once exclaimed to her sisters: "Let us all, full of holy desire, hasten to venerate the sweetest Countenance of Our Lord, which will in Heaven be our *all*—all that a glorified soul can desire." On one occasion when this saint had asked Our Lord to grant that those who celebrate the memory of His sweet Face should never be deprived of His amiable company, He replied in these precious words: "*Not one of them shall be separated from Me.*" (Bk. I, ch. xiii). The Lord then pronounced this blessing: "The splendor of My Countenance be their eternal rejoicing."

## St. Edmund

The great servant of God, St. Edmund of Canterbury, was accustomed to pray: "May I expire from ardent desire of beholding the Face of Our Lord Jesus Christ."

# St. Therese of the Child Jesus And of the Holy Face

The dear Carmelite saint, Therese of the Child Jesus and of the Holy Face, more familiarly known as "The Little Flower," who died September 30, 1897, nourished a touching, ardent devotion to the Adorable Countenance of our Saviour. She sought to soothe the sufferings of the Holy Face by bringing Our Lord sacrifices to save souls, and she encouraged others to do likewise. She composed a most beautiful prayer in honor of the Holy Face and recited it daily. This prayer reveals her compassion for Jesus in His sufferings, as well as her vehement longing to behold His Divine Face in glory. Veneration of the Holy Face was one of her dearest devotions. After Holy Communion she would, in spirit, bend over the Face of her Beloved, which delighted her with Its secret charms.

## The Carmelite Nun of Tours

On July 8, 1848, Sister Mary of St. Peter died in the odor of sanctity in the Carmelite Convent of Tours in France. She had been favored by Heaven with many revelations concerning the reparation of blasphemies uttered against the Holy Name of Jesus, and veneration of the Holy Face had been pointed out to her as a most efficacious means of making such reparation. Our Divine Saviour transported her in spirit to the spot where He was met by Veronica, on His way to Calvary, and made known to His spouse how great was the service this heroic woman had rendered Him when, with her veil, she wiped His Adorable Face, all covered with spittle, dust, perspiration and blood.

Our Saviour revealed to this religious how great is the satisfaction He derives from the veneration of His Sacred Countenance, saying: "According to the care you take in making reparation to My Face, disfigured by blasphemers, so will I take care of yours which has been disfigured by sin. I will reprint upon it My image and render it as beautiful as it was on leaving the baptismal font."

At another time Our Lord said to Sister Mary of St. Peter, "I seek pious souls who, like Veronica, will wipe My Divine Countenance and venerate It. . . . Those who on earth venerate My wounded Countenance will once behold It in Heaven all resplendent in glory."

Again Jesus said to His spouse: "All who honor My Holy Face in a spirit of reparation thereby perform for Me the services of the pious Veronica."

Devotion to the Holy Face is regarded as a sign of predestination, for how were it possible that a soul who had loved this Divine Countenance here on earth would be excluded from beholding It in glory in Heaven!

## Chapter 4

### Promises in Favor of All Who Honor The Holy Face of Our Saviour

1. "All those who meditate frequently on the vision of My Divine Face, attracted by the desires of love, shall receive within them, by the virtue of My Humanity, a bright ray of My Divinity, which shall enlighten their inmost souls, so that they shall reflect the light of My Countenance in a special manner throughout eternity."—Our Lord to St. Gertrude

2. Our Lord, having been asked by St. Mechtilde to grant that those who celebrate the memory of His sweet Face should never be deprived of His amiable company, replied: "Not one of them shall be separated from Me."

*The following are taken from the writings of Sister Mary of St. Peter:*

3. "Our Lord has promised me that He will imprint His Divine likeness on the souls of those who honor His Holy Face." (January 21, 1847). "This Adorable Face is, as it were, the seal of the Divinity, which has the virtue of reproducing in souls God's image." (November 6, 1845).

4. "By My Holy Face you shall work miracles." (October 27, 1845).

5. "By My Holy Face you will obtain the conversion of numberless sinners. Nothing that you ask in making this offering will be refused you. Oh, if you but knew how pleasing is the sight of My Face to My Heavenly Father!" (November 22, 1846).

6. "As you can procure in a kingdom all you wish through a coin marked with the king's effigy, so in the Kingdom of Heaven will you obtain all your desires through the precious coin of My holy Humanity, which is My Adorable Countenance." (October 29, 1845).

7. "According to the care you take in making reparation to My Face, disfigured by blasphemers, so will I take care of yours which has been disfigured by sin. I will reprint upon it My image and render it

as beautiful as it was on leaving the baptismal font." (November 3, 1845).

8. "Our Saviour has promised me," said Sister Mary of St. Peter, "that He will defend before His Father all who in this work of reparation defend His cause by word, prayer or writing; that at their death He will purify their souls, effacing all stain of sin, and restore to them their primitive beauty." (March 12, 1846).

How wonderful and consoling are these promises!

## Chapter 5

## Meditations on the Holy Face

FREQUENT mention is made of the Face of God in the Old Testament. "Show us Thy Face, O Lord, and we shall be saved," cries the Psalmist. The Angels and Saints adore this Face in Heaven; the Patriarchs, Prophets and just of all ages have contemplated It with profound veneration and religious awe. But when the Second Person of the Most Blessed Trinity, the Word, was made Man, the Divine Face became in the Person of Jesus Christ an object of admiration, respect and love.

How charming was the human Countenance of Him whose *eternal, uncreated beauty fills all Heaven with eternal bliss!* Men beheld with admiration the Son of God incarnate. Most profound humility, most exalted purity, most tender love, most sublime majesty beamed from His Divine Face, for, as St. Paul writes, "The goodness and

kindness of God our Saviour hath appeared."
(*Titus* 3:4). In beauty and perfection He
surpassed all the children of men.

## The Adorable Face in Childhood

Oh, with what sentiments must the
Blessed Virgin Mary have gazed into the
Countenance of her newborn Infant as He
lay in the manger! This Infant reflected the
*splendor,* the *sanctity,* the *majesty of God,*
but likewise the beauty, the holiness and
the sweetness of His virgin Mother. With
Mary and Joseph, let us gaze upon the
sweet, radiant Face of this amiable Child,
the "most beautiful of the sons of men." As
the Psalmist wrote: "Thou art beautiful
above the sons of men . . ." (*Ps.* 44(45): 3).

For two thousand years the Patriarchs
and Prophets had desired to see this Face.
"Lord, show us Thy Face and we shall be
saved" was their unceasing prayer. At
length this Face appeared! See how beautiful and amiable It is! Its first tears, Its
first smiles are for our salvation. With the
Prophet let us exclaim: "The light of Thy
Countenance, O Lord, is signed upon us:
Thou hast given gladness in my heart."
(*Ps.* 4:7).

# The Adorable Face in Manhood

Contemplate, in all the stages of His life, the Divine Countenance of our Saviour, the august Face of the God-man, the mirror of the holiest of souls and the most tender of hearts. That Face ravished the multitudes; It attracted the Apostles; It gazed with compassion on the afflicted; It bent a look of mercy on sinners. *Light, grace, pardon, life ever beamed* like rays from the *Adorable Face.*

Behold the Divine Face transfigured on Thabor, when It reflected but a passing ray of the eternal splendor, distilled but a drop of that ocean of felicity of which the Face of the Lord is the inexhaustible source.

Truly, the Sacred Countenance of our Saviour, in all the stages of His life, merits our contemplation and adoration, but more especially in the humiliation and pains to which It was subjected in His Passion.

## The Holy Face in the Garden of Olives

When Jesus was agonizing in the Garden of Olives, He prostrated Himself with His face to the ground. Untold anguish was depicted on His Adorable Countenance. Three times He raised His eyes to Heaven to His Father, three times His quivering lips prayed in sorrow: "Father, if Thou wilt, remove this chalice from Me. . . . Nevertheless, not as I will, but as Thou wilt." The heavenly beauty of His Sacred Face was dimmed by the bloody sweat and finally defiled by the traitorous kiss of Judas.

## The Holy Face during the Crowning with Thorns

To what countless insults was the Adorable Face of Jesus exposed during His scourging and crowning with thorns! There was no species of insult and suffering to which Jesus did not submit His Holy Face during this part of His bitter Passion. His head and forehead were crowned with thorns, His eyes bathed in tears and filled with blood, while blows, spittle and the most savage outrages were inflicted upon His Adorable Face. "There is no beauty in Him," says the Prophet, "nor comeliness: and we have seen Him, and there is no sightliness, that we should be desirous of Him. Despised, and the most abject of men, a man of sorrows." (*Is.* 53:2-3). "Then did they spit in His Face, and buffeted Him: and others struck His Face with the palms of their hands," writes St. Matthew. (*Matt.* 26:67).

The same Divine Countenance which on Mount Thabor had shone like the sun, and upon which the Angels desire to gaze, is now treated with the most shameful insolence, is struck and spit upon! How the words of the Messias by the mouth of the Prophet Isaias are here verified: "I have given My body to the strikers, and My cheeks to them that plucked them: I have not turned away My Face from them that rebuked Me, and spit upon Me." (*Is.* 50:6).

Surely it was not without design that God permitted these minute and touching details to be transmitted to us in Holy Writ. It was not without reason that Jesus imprinted the likeness of His agonizing Countenance on Veronica's veil, as He bore His Cross to Calvary. Evidently Our Lord's intention was to turn our thoughts with special tenderness and love toward the sufferings of His Adorable Face while we meditate on the mysteries of His Passion. Amid all this ignominious and cruel treatment, what patience was shown on the part of our dear Saviour! He complained not; He murmured not. His Adorable Face retained Its heavenly serenity, Its ineffable sweetness.

## *Ecce Homo!*—Behold the Man!

How unspeakable must have been the pain caused by the thorns which encircled the Adorable Head of our Saviour! Ah, what a spectacle when Pilate presented Jesus to the populace with the words: "*Ecce Homo!*"—"Behold the Man!" Blood filled His eyes, stained His lips, clotted His beard and made Him wholly unrecognizable. His whole body was one mass of stripes and wounds. Oh, soul-crushing sight! Jesus stood with downcast eyes, but the anguish of His Heart was clearly depicted on His Face when He heard the murderous cry: "Crucify Him! Crucify Him!"

# The Agonizing Face of Jesus On the Cross

Behold Jesus in untold agony on the Cross. From His head, heavy with that awful crown, rivulets of blood flow down into His eyes, over His beard and into His languishing mouth. His Adorable Face is now bowed low upon His breast and cannot raise Itself under that wide-circling crown of thorns without unspeakable suffering. See Him lift His tearful eyes to the Heavenly Father and entreat pardon for us: "Father, forgive them, for they know not what they do."

Seven times those parched and burning lips are opened to speak words of pardon and blessing. Jesus turns His forgiving, suffering eyes upon the good thief who has implored mercy, and says: "This day thou shalt be with Me in paradise." He looks upon His Mother with an earnest, compassionate gaze, then turns His eyes toward the beloved disciple, John, and says: "Woman, behold thy son. . . . Son, behold thy Mother." His Holy Face gradually becomes pale, livid and bloodless, and from His agonizing Heart escapes the cry: "My

God, My God, *why hast Thou forsaken Me?*" Utterly exhausted, consumed by a thirst caused by the fever of many wounds, His tongue parched, our Saviour exclaims: "I thirst!"

Now His death agony begins. A cold sweat breaks out over His body and covers His sacred brow. But Mary, the tenderest of Mothers, cannot soothe her dying Son by wiping that death sweat from His forehead. How anxiously she watches as His Face becomes drawn and His cheeks sunken, as He drops His chin, opens His blood-filled eyes and raises His thorn-crowned head. Her heart is rent with grief as she hears His anguished cry: "It is consummated!" Then He raises His Adorable Head, and for the last time His weeping Mother hears her Son's voice: "Father, into Thy hands I commend My spirit."

His sufferings are over. His Adorable Head drops on His breast and He gives up the ghost. Oh, how terrible was the agony on the Cross! What swords must have penetrated the soul of the virgin Mother while beholding the Face of her Adorable Son distorted in such heart-rending agony.

# The Holy Face in Death

After the lifeless body of Jesus had been taken down from the Cross, His head rested upon Mary's knee. Oh, how tenderly, how sorrowfully she pressed her lips to that Sacred Face! A privileged soul beheld in vision how the Dolorous Mother lovingly cut away the cruel crown and plucked out the thorns which had pierced the Sacred Head; how she tenderly washed the blood from the wounds of our Saviour's head and let her tear-stained face sink sadly down upon His.

St. Ephrem, compassionating the Dolorous Mother holding her Divine Son, places these words on her lips: "I kiss the wounds of my dearest Son and my God. I salute my own Child, I embrace my Son's body; I kiss His most sweet mouth, His eyes, His Face, His hands and feet, and His most Precious Blood so cruelly and unjustly shed. O my Son, my most sweet and dearest Son, I honor Thee in Thy death. See, the sword has pierced my heart through and through! See my wounds, my Son and my God!" Let us imitate Mary in venerating the Holy Face in death.

## The Glorious Face in the Resurrection

Behold Jesus gloriously risen, triumphant over death and Hell, coming forth from the sepulchre, impassible and incorruptible. His Holy Face is shining with glory and immortality, radiantly beautiful in Its triumphant splendor. What celestial fire in His eyes! What serenity on His brow! What majesty in His Countenance! His Sacred Face is the brightness of eternal light, the unspotted mirror of God's majesty, the image of His goodness. It dazzles us with Its splendor; our hearts rejoice to see It inundated with joy.

When the Apostles, assembled in the Cenacle, saw the Face of our risen Saviour for the first time, "they wondered for joy," says the Evangelist. Our Lord's look of tenderness, His smile, His kind paternal words, His very breath filled them with inexpressible peace and happiness such as they had never before experienced.

# The Glorious Face in Heaven

Oh, what is the joy of the elect as they behold, in all Its undimmed splendor, the glorious Face of the Incarnate Word! Oh, wondrous sight that enables them to see, as in a clear mirror, the secrets of the Divine Essence! They see that most Holy Face in all Its radiant beauty, as It is in reality, and they are made like unto It.

O Lord, permit us to behold Thee and to see Thy Face in all Its glory throughout eternity! Then, indeed, will our hearts be satiated with joy. "Then," says St. Augustine, "free from all care, we shall see, we shall love, we shall praise. We shall see the ineffably beautiful Face of the Divine King; *we shall love the sweet and amiable Face of the Son of God and the Son of Mary;* we shall praise the victorious, powerful Face of the Redeemer. We shall behold It forever; we shall love It rapturously; we shall praise It without weariness and with ever-reviving transports, ever-renewed joy, forever and ever. Amen."

## Chapter 6

## Veneration of the Sacred Face
## In the Blessed Sacrament

OUR dear Saviour admonished St. Mechtilde to render all possible honor to His Adorable Heart in the Blessed Sacrament. His delight will be equally great if pious souls cherish a special devotion to His Holy Face in the Adorable Eucharist.

Loving souls should, with the eye of faith, contemplate the Blessed Countenance of Our Lord in the Sacred Host. As often as we cast a reverent look upon the Sacred Host, and hence also upon the Divine Countenance hidden there, Our Lord looks upon us, and we merit an additional degree of glory in Heaven. St. Gertrude was vouchsafed a marvelous revelation which souls should not fail to take to heart, because there is question of gaining unspeakable merits. This privileged saint received from God the assurance that whenever anyone reverently looks at the Sacred Host, which is the very Body and Blood of Christ, He will add another degree to the glory which awaits the soul in Heaven; also, that He would impart to the soul, when it attains to the Beatific Vision of God, as many special delights as it has cast reverent looks at the Sacred Host.

We should, therefore, exert ourselves *to see the Sacred Host whenever It is exposed to view,* and turn our spiritual eye to the *hidden Face* of Jesus Christ. It is also very pleasing to Our Lord if we salute His Adorable Face, especially in the Blessed Sacrament. St. Gertrude was accustomed to salute each member of Our Lord's Body, and whenever she did so, splendor appeared to emanate from the sacred member thus saluted and to irradiate her whole soul. In that splendor she was clothed with the innocence which Our Lord acquired for us by the sufferings of that particular member of His body.

After Holy Communion let us, in spirit, bend down and reverently kiss the Sacred Countenance of Jesus. Sometimes let us lovingly venerate His infant features; at other times, the Countenance of our thorn-crowned Saviour; again, the Face of our most faithful Friend or our loving, amiable Bridegroom. If we frequently venerate the Holy Face of Jesus thus, He will sanctify our own countenance, the looks of our eyes and the words of our lips; He will purify our thoughts and give us grace not to offend Him by our senses, but to use them only for His glory.

Devotion to the Holy Face is, indeed, *a consoling devotion:* consoling in life, in death and after death. Especially when we stand before the Judgment seat of God shall our veneration of the Sacred Face be rewarded; for, having devoutly honored the Holy Countenance in life, surely we may hope that then Jesus will look upon us tenderly and lovingly and render to us a merciful judgment.

## Chapter 7

## Power of the Holy Face Over Sinners

THE effect of our Saviour's look upon the Apostle St. Peter furnishes an example of the virtue of the Holy Face in touching souls. The sight of that sorrowful Face, the light of those sad, tender eyes, that gaze of gentle reproach, compassion and love pierced the Apostle's heart and filled him with shame and repentance.

St. Vincent de Paul once sought vainly to convert a sinner. At length, presenting a picture of the Holy Face to the dissolute youth, he said, "I entreat you to look at this picture for one moment every evening before you retire."

"Is that all?" interrupted the young man, laughing.

"Nothing more; that will suffice," replied Vincent de Paul with an earnest smile, and the saint and sinner parted.

The first night, the sinner laid the image

aside unmoved. The second night, it seemed more pitiable. Soon he found it tedious always to look at the same picture, but he continued to do so eight, ten, twelve days, because he had promised St. Vincent he would do so. On the 13th day, changed and contrite, he sought the Saint and exclaimed: "I wish to go to Confession. I can bear it no longer! The Countenance of my Saviour, streaming with blood and tears, reproaches me too bitterly! I will return to God and make my peace with Him." And he remained true to his resolution.

Hippolitus, a pious priest of Florence, had a painting made of our thorn-crowned Saviour and hung it in his room near a window. Before this image he often stood for a long time, meditating upon the infinite love which had constrained Our Lord to suffer so much for us. This meditation proved for him the most fruitful source of holy thoughts and pious resolutions.

Directly opposite his house there lived a vain, self-conceited woman who often saw the priest standing long before what she thought was a mirror. At length, to satisfy her curiosity, she ventured to ask the priest to show her the mirror in which he so often viewed himself. The priest consented and brought her the painting, that she might gaze into this new mirror to her heart's content and see herself as she truly was.

What was her amazement, even fright, when, instead of a crystal mirror, she beheld the *Ecce Homo!* She was much embarrassed, yet she could not turn her eyes from the touching image. There her gaze rested upon the head of Our Lord encircled with a crown of thorns, with mournful eyes and pale, sad Face. The priest profited by this opportunity to admonish the worldly woman, and said: "Behold here the mirror in which you, too, should daily contemplate yourself. See our poor Saviour, for love of us so basely maltreated! Will you, too, remain cold as did the Jews to whom Pilate presented the lacerated Jesus, crying out, 'Behold the Man!'? As this Countenance of our Redeemer is disfigured by wounds, so is your soul disfigured by sin. Wash your soul with tears of compunction, and instead of this sad and disfigured image, you will one day behold and admire the glorified Countenance of the Divine Saviour eternally in Heaven." These words impressed the heart of the

sinner. From that hour she led a peniten-
tial life.

For us, too, dear Christian, the image of
the thorn-crowned Christ is a most instruc-
tive mirror. If one would look upon an
image of the Holy Face daily, and then say
his prayers, he would certainly become
milder, purer, nobler, more serious, more
charitable. The impression made by the
image would compel him to do so.

## *Chapter 8*

# Prayers

### Mass in Honor of the Most Holy Face Of Our Lord Jesus Christ Disfigured in His Passion

*Introit.* For Thy glory, O Lord, I have suffered opprobrium; My Face has been covered with confusion and I have become a mockery to them. *Ps.* Save me, O God, because the waters of tribulation have entered into my soul. *V.* Glory be to the Father . . .

*Collect.* Grant, we beseech Thee, almighty and merciful God, that whilst venerating the Face of Thy Christ, disfigured in the

Passion because of our sins, we may merit to contemplate It shining forever in celestial glory. Through the same Lord . . .

***Epistle (Is. 53).*** As many have been astonished at Thee, so shall His visage be inglorious among men, and His form among the sons of men. He shall sprinkle many nations; kings shall shut their mouths at Him: for they to whom it was not told of Him, have seen: and they that had not heard, have beheld. Who hath believed our report? And to whom is the arm of the Lord revealed? And He shall grow up as a tender plant before Him, and as a root out of a thirsty ground. There is no beauty in Him, nor comeliness. And we have seen Him, and there was no sightliness, that we should be desirous of Him: despised, and the most abject of men, a man of sorrows, and acquainted with infirmity. And His look was as it were hidden and despised, whereupon we esteemed Him not. Surely He hath borne our infirmities and carried our sorrows.

***Gradual.*** The confusion of My Face hath covered Me at the voice of him that reproacheth and detracteth Me: at the face of the enemy and persecutor. *V.* And some began to spit on Him, to cover His Face, and to buffet Him, and to say unto Him: Prophesy. And the servants struck Him with the palms of their hands.

**Tract.** My Heart hath expected reproach and misery. And I looked for one that would grieve together with Me, but there was none; and for one that would comfort Me, and I found none. And they gave Me gall for My food, and in My thirst they gave Me vinegar to drink. *V.* They have persecuted Him whom Thou hast smitten; and they have added to the grief of my wounds.

**Gospel (Mark 14:61-65).** At that time the high priest questioned Jesus and said to Him: Art Thou the Christ, the Son of the Blessed God? But Jesus said to him: I am; and you shall see the Son of Man sitting on the right hand of the power of God, and coming with the clouds of heaven. Then the high priest, rending his garments, said: What need we any further witnesses? You have heard the blasphemy. What think you? Who all condemned Him to be guilty of death.

And some began to spit upon Him, and to cover His Face, and to buffet Him, and to say unto Him: Prophesy. And the servants struck Him with the palms of their hands.

***Offertory.*** A false speaker riseth up against My Face, contradicting Me. They have opened their mouths upon Me, and reproaching Me, they have struck Me on the cheek; they are filled with My pains. These things have I suffered when I offered pure prayers to God.

***Secret.*** O God of mercy, turn away Thy Face from our crimes and cast Thine eyes upon the Face of Thy Christ, who hath offered Himself to Thee as a Victim for us, and hath washed us from our sins in His own Blood. Through the same Jesus Christ . . .

***Preface.*** It is truly meet and just, right and availing unto salvation, that we should always and in all places give thanks unto Thee, holy Lord, Father almighty, everlasting God; Who didst set the salvation of mankind upon the tree of the cross, so that whence came death, thence also life might rise again; and he that overcame by the

tree, on the tree also might be overcome:
through Christ Our Lord. Through whom
the Angels praise Thy Majesty, the Domin-
ions worship it, and the Powers are in awe.
The heavenly hosts and the blessed
Seraphim join together in celebrating their
joy. With these we pray Thee join our own
voices also, while we say with lowly praise:
Holy, holy, holy . . .

*Communion.* Let us go forth from the
camp, and let us go to Jesus, bearing the
ignominy of His cross.

*Postcommunion.* Deign, O Lord, to grant
to those who adore Thy Face, once hidden
under the ignominy of the Passion and now
veiled in the Sacrament of Thy love, grace
to compensate Thee by their homage for
Thy opprobrium upon earth, and to merit
a share in Thy glory in Heaven. Who livest
and reignest . . .

# Invocations of the Holy Face

*Approved for private use by Pope Pius IX,
January 27, 1853.*

—I—

O Jesus, whose Adorable Face Mary and
Joseph worshipped with profoundest
reverence, *have mercy on us.*

O Jesus, whose Adorable Face ravished
with joy the Angels, shepherds and
Magi in the stable of Bethlehem, *have
mercy on us.*

O Jesus, whose Adorable Face wounded with
a dart of love the aged Simeon and the
Prophetess Anna in the Temple, *etc.*

O Jesus, whose Adorable Face was bathed
in tears in Thy holy infancy,

O Jesus, whose Adorable Face at the age
of twelve astonished the doctors in the
Temple,

O Jesus, whose Adorable Face is white with
purity and ruddy with charity,

O Jesus, whose Adorable Face is more
beautiful than the sun, brighter than
the moon and more brilliant than the
stars,

O Jesus, whose Adorable Face is lovelier
than the roses of spring,

O Jesus, whose Adorable Face is more precious than gold, silver and gems,

O Jesus, the charms and grace of whose Adorable Face win all hearts,

O Jesus, whose Adorable Face is most noble in Its heavenly features,

O Jesus, whose Adorable Face is the admiration of angels,

O Jesus, whose Adorable Face is the sweet delight of the Saints,

O Jesus, whose Adorable Face is the masterpiece of the Holy Ghost in which the Father is well pleased,

O Jesus, whose Adorable Face was the delight of Thy Virgin Mother and of Thy holy foster father St. Joseph,

O Jesus, whose Adorable Face is the ineffable mirror of Divine perfections,

O Jesus, the beauty of whose Adorable Face is ever ancient and ever new,

O Jesus, whose Adorable Face appeases the Divine wrath,

O Jesus, whose Adorable Face is the terror of the evil spirits,

O Jesus, whose Adorable Face is the treasure of graces and blessings,

O Jesus, whose Adorable Face was exposed to the inclemency of the weather in the desert,

O Jesus, whose Adorable Face was scorched
by the sun and bathed in sweat on
Thy journeys,

O Jesus, the expression of whose Adorable
Face is wholly Divine,

O Jesus, the modesty and mildness of
whose Adorable Face attracted both
the just and sinners,

O Jesus, whose Adorable Face gave a holy
kiss and blessing to the little children,

O Jesus, whose Adorable Face sorrowed and
wept at the grave of Lazarus,

O Jesus, whose Adorable Face was brilliant
as the sun and radiant with glory on
Mount Thabor,

V. The light of Thy Face has been shed
upon us, O Lord;
R. *Thou hast given joy to our hearts.*

### *Let Us Pray*

I salute Thee, I adore Thee, I love Thee,
O Adorable Face of Jesus, my Beloved, noble
seal of the Divinity! With all the powers of
my soul, I apply myself to Thee and most
humbly pray Thee to imprint in us all the
features of Thy Divine likeness. Amen.

—II—

O Jesus, whose Adorable Face grew sad at
the sight of Jerusalem and wept over
that ungrateful city, *have mercy on us.*

O Jesus, whose Adorable Face bowed to the
earth in the Garden of Olives because
of the burden of our sins, *have mercy
on us.*

O Jesus, whose Adorable Face was bathed
in bloody sweat, *etc.*

O Jesus, whose Adorable Face was kissed
by Judas, the traitor,

O Jesus, the power of whose Adorable Face
smote the soldiers to the ground in
the Garden of Olives,

O Jesus, whose Adorable Face was struck
by a vile servant, derided by enemies
and desecrated by their unholy hands,

O Jesus, whose Adorable Face was defiled
with spittle and bruised by blows,

O Jesus, the Divine look of whose Adorable
Face wounded Peter's heart with love
and sorrow,

O Jesus, whose Adorable Face was hum-
bled for us before the tribunals of
Jerusalem,

O Jesus, whose Adorable Face preserved Its

attractiveness and dignity when Pilate pronounced the death sentence,

O Jesus, the brow of whose Adorable Face was crowned with thorns,

O Jesus, whose Adorable Face was covered with bloody sweat which fell to the ground under the Cross,

O Jesus, whose Adorable Face is worthy of all our reverence, veneration and worship,

O Jesus, whose Adorable Face the pious Veronica wiped on the way to Calvary,

O Jesus, whose Adorable Face was lifted up on the torturous Cross,

O Jesus, the eyes of whose Adorable Face shed tears of blood,

O Jesus, the mouth of whose Adorable Face was tormented with vinegar and gall,

O Jesus, the hair and beard of whose Adorable Face were plucked out by the executioners,

O Jesus, whose Adorable Face was disfigured like to that of a leper,

O Jesus, the incomparable beauty of whose Adorable Face was disfigured by the sins of the world,

O Jesus, whose Adorable Face was overcast by the mournful shadows of death,

O Jesus, whose Adorable Face was washed,
  anointed and wrapped in a shroud by
  Mary and the holy women,
O Jesus, whose Adorable Face was laid to
  rest in the grave,
O Jesus, whose Adorable Face was resplen-
  dent in beauty on the day of Thy
  Resurrection,
O Jesus, whose Adorable Face was radiant
  in glory on the day of Thine Ascension,
O Jesus, whose Adorable Face is hidden in
  the Most Blessed Sacrament of the
  Altar,
O Jesus, whose Adorable Face will appear
  on the clouds in great power and
  majesty at the end of the world,
O Jesus, whose Adorable Face will be the
  terror of sinners,
O Jesus, whose Adorable Face is the joy of
  the just in Heaven,

V. O Lord, show us Thy Face,
R. *And we shall be saved.*

### *Let Us Pray*

We beseech Thee, O Almighty and merciful God, grant us and all who venerate
the Countenance of Thy dearly beloved

Son, all disfigured by our sins, the grace
to behold It throughout eternity in the glory
of Its majesty, through the same Jesus
Christ Our Lord. Amen.

## Praises of the Holy Face

Blessed be Jesus!

Blessed be the Holy Face of Jesus!

Blessed be the Holy Face in the majesty
and beauty of Its heavenly features!

Blessed be the Holy Face through the words
which issued from Its Divine mouth!

Blessed be the Holy Face through all the
glances of Its Adorable eyes!

Blessed be the Holy Face in the transfiguration of Thabor!

Blessed be the Holy Face in the fatigues of
Its apostolate!

Blessed be the Holy Face in the bloody
sweat of the agony!

Blessed be the Holy Face in the humiliations of the Passion!

Blessed be the Holy Face in the sufferings
of death!

Blessed be the Holy Face in the splendor
of the Resurrection!

Blessed be the Holy Face in the glory of
light eternal!

## Benediction of
## St. Francis of Assisi
## Through the Holy Face

The Lord bless thee and keep thee;
The Lord show His Face to thee and have
    mercy on thee;
The Lord turn His Countenance to thee,
    and give thee peace. (*Num.* 6:24-27).

## Salutations to the Holy Face in
## the Blessed Sacrament

HAIL O Adorable Face of Jesus, present in the Most Blessed Sacrament, more resplendent than the sun! Hail Thou noble seal of the Divinity, Thou mirror of Divine perfections! With all the powers of my soul I turn to Thee, O Jesus, and humbly pray Thee to imprint upon our hearts all the features of Thy Divine Countenance. Amen.

## Prayer to the Holy Face

*Composed by St. Therese of the Child Jesus
and of the Holy Face—
"The Little Flower of Jesus"*

O JESUS, Who in Thy Cruel Passion didst become "the reproach of men and the Man of Sorrows," I worship Thy Divine Face. Once it shone with the beauty and sweetness of the Divinity; now for my sake It is become as the face of a leper. Yet in that disfigured Countenance I recognize Thine infinite love, and I am consumed with the desire of loving Thee and of making Thee loved by all mankind. The tears that streamed in such abundance from Thine eyes are to me as precious pearls which I delight to gather, that with their infinite worth I may ransom the souls of poor sinners.

O Jesus, Whose Face is the sole beauty that ravishes my heart, I may not behold here upon earth the sweetness of Thy glance, nor feel the ineffable tenderness of Thy kiss. Thereto I consent, but pray Thee to imprint in me Thy Divine likeness; and I implore Thee so to inflame me with Thy love that it may quickly consume me, and that I may reach the vision of Thy glorious Face in Heaven. Amen.

## Act of Love to the Holy Face

ADORABLE Face of my Jesus, my only love, my light and my life, grant that I may see, know and love Thee alone, that I may live with Thee, of Thee and for Thee. Amen.

## Veneration of the Thorn-Crowned Head of Our Saviour

*"And platting a crown of thorns, they put it upon His head. . . . They began to spit upon Him, and they gave Him blows. Others smote His face and said: 'Prophesy, who is it that struck Thee?'"*

O HOLY Redeemer! Thou art clothed with a scarlet cloak, a reed is placed in Thy hand for a scepter, and the sharp points of a thorny crown are pressed into Thine adorable head.

My soul, thou canst never conceive the sufferings, the insults and the indignities offered to our Blessed Lord during this scene of pain and mockery.

The Jews mock Thee, O Jesus. I salute Thee and offer Thee supreme homage as

King of Heaven and earth, the Redeemer of the world, the Eternal Son of the Living God.

O my afflicted Saviour! O King of the world! Thou art ridiculed as a mock king; I believe in Thee and adore Thee as the King of kings and Lord of lords, as the supreme Ruler of Heaven and earth.

O Jesus! I devoutly venerate Thy sacred head pierced with thorns, struck with a reed, overwhelmed with pain and derision.

I adore the Precious Blood flowing from Thy bleeding wounds. To Thee be all praise, all thanksgiving and all love for evermore!

O meek Lamb, Victim for sin! May Thy thorns penetrate my heart with fervent love, that I may never cease to adore Thee as my God, my King and my Saviour.

V. Behold, O God, our protector,
R. *And look upon the Face of Thy Christ.*

### *Let Us Pray*

O my beloved Saviour, at the sight of Thy most Holy Face disfigured by suffering, at the sight of Thy Sacred Heart so full of love, I cry out with St. Augustine: "Lord Jesus, imprint on my heart Thy sacred wounds, so that I may read therein sorrow and love: sorrow, to endure every sorrow for Thee; love, to despise every love for Thee. Amen."

## Ecce Homo!

*"Jesus therefore came forth bearing the crown of thorns and the purple garment. And Pilate saith to them: 'Behold the man.'"*

HASTEN hither, O my soul, and behold thy Saviour; behold in how pitiable a condition He is presented to the people.

Behold how the glory of the Eternal Father, the Mirror of His splendor, has become disfigured.

Behold your Redeemer: the crown of thorns upon His head, the blood streaming down His Face; His hands, swollen and cut by the cords, holding a reed instead of a scepter; the mock mantle saturated by the bleeding wounds of His torn and mangled body!

O bleeding Jesus, to what an agonizing state Thou art reduced! Thou, the most beautiful of the children of men, hast become a man of sorrows.

Hail Adorable Face, worthy of all respect, veneration and worship! O worshipful Face, whose brow is crowned with thorns, whose eyes are filled with blood!

We venerate Thee, O Adorable Face, into whose mouth is poured vinegar and gall, whose hair and beard are painfully torn out.

V. Show us Thy Face,
R. *And we shall be saved.*

### Let Us Pray

Almighty and merciful God, grant, we beseech Thee, that while reverencing the Face of Thy Christ, disfigured in the Passion because of our sins, we may merit to contemplate It shining forever in celestial glory; through the same Jesus Christ Our Lord. Amen.

## Prayers to the Holy Face

I SALUTE Thee, I adore Thee, and I love Thee, O Jesus my Saviour, outraged anew by blasphemers; and I offer Thee, through the heart of Thy Blessed Mother, the worship of all the Angels and Saints as an incense and a sweet perfume,

most humbly beseeching Thee, by virtue of
Thy Sacred Face, to repair and renew, in
me and in all men, Thine image disfigured
by sin. Amen.
*Our Father ... Hail Mary ... Glory be ...*

O ADORABLE Face of my Jesus, so
mercifully bowed down upon the
tree of the Cross on the day Thou
didst die for the salvation of man, now
again incline in Thy pity toward us poor
sinners; cast upon us a look of compassion,
and receive us to the kiss of peace. Amen.

Sacred Heart of Jesus, have mercy on us.
Amen.

## O Sacred Head

O Head, all gashed and gory!
O'erwhelmed in woe and scorn;
O Head, the Angels' glory!
Yet pierced by many a thorn.
Far other fate should meet Thee,
Far other be Thy crown;
A thousand times I greet Thee,
While tears of love flow down.

Thy cheeks are wan and faded,
Thy lips are ghastly white,
Thy beauty quite o'ershaded
In death's obscurest night.
Yet tender love is lighting
E'en still Thy Sacred Face,
Poor sinners still inviting
To undeserved grace.

Ah, Lord, the thorns Thou wearest
Should pierce my guilty brow;
Beneath the Cross Thou bearest
My sinful back should bow;
The cru-el whips that tore Thee,
Mine, mine alone should be;
Yet, Jesus, I implore Thee,
Turn not Thy Face from me.

When my last hour is knelling
Forsake me not, I pray;
But shades of death dispelling,
Be Thou my light, my stay.
O Face, now gashed and gory!
What joy it is to me,
To hope one day in glory
Thy gracious smile to see.

# Prayer of Reparation to the Holy Face

O LORD Jesus! After contemplating Thy features, disfigured by grief; after meditating upon Thy Passion with compunction and love, how can our hearts fail to be inflamed with a holy hatred of sin, which even now outrages Thine Adorable Face? Lord, suffer us not to be content with mere compassion, but give us grace so closely to follow Thee on this new Calvary, that the opprobrium destined for Thee may fall upon us, O Jesus; that thus we may have a share, small though it be, in the expiation of sin. Amen.

# Offering of the Holy Face to the Eternal Father

ALMIGHTY God, Eternal Father, contemplate the Face of Thy Son, Our Lord Jesus Christ. Most confidently do we present It to Thee for the glory of Thy Holy Name, the exaltation of Thy Holy Church, and the salvation of the world. Our Advocate most merciful, He opens His mouth to plead our cause; listen to His cries, behold His tears, O my God, and Thou wilt be touched with compassion for sinners who implore Thy grace and mercy. Amen.

## Prayer of Bl. Pope Pius IX

O MY JESUS! Cast upon us a look of mercy; turn Thy Face upon each one of, even as Thou didst upon Veronica; not that we may see It with the eyes of our body, for we do not deserve this; but turn It toward our hearts, that being sustained by Thee, we may draw from that powerful source strength for the combats we must ever wage on earth.

Eternal Father, we offer Thee the Adorable Face of Thy Well-Beloved Son for the honor and glory of Thy Holy Name and for the salvation of all men.

## Prayer of St. Augustine

I APPEAR before Thy Holy Face, O my Saviour, laden with my sins and the penalties they have brought upon me. What I suffer is far less than I deserve, for although conscious of the justice of my punishment, I cease not on that account to commit fresh sins every day. I sink beneath Thy scourges, yet I do not amend my ways; my heart is full of bitterness, still my obstinacy in evil remains ever the same. My life is spent in misery, and I do not correct myself. When Thou chastisest me, I make Thee great promises, which, as soon as Thou liftest up Thy hand, I forget.

I come now to make to Thee, O God, a sincere confession of my sins. I declare in Thy presence that if Thou show not Thy mercy to me, I shall surely perish. Grant me, my Saviour, what I beg of Thee, since of Thy pure goodness Thou hast drawn me out of nothingness to put me into a state wherein I can pray to Thee. Amen.

## Salutations

Hail, Adorable Head, crowned with thorns and struck with the reed for us!

Hail, worshipful Face, spit upon and smitten for us!

# Prayer to Our Lord on the Cross For a Happy Hour of Death

O MY CRUCIFIED JESUS, mercifully accept the prayer which I now make to Thee for help in the moment of my death, when at its approach all my senses shall fail me.

When, therefore, O sweetest Jesus, my weary and downcast eyes can no longer look up to Thee, be mindful of the loving gaze which now I turn on Thee, and have mercy on me.

When my parched lips can no longer kiss Thy most sacred wounds, remember then those kisses which now I imprint on Thee, and have mercy on me.

When my cold hands can no longer embrace Thy cross, forget not the affection with which I embrace it now, and have mercy on me.

And when, at length, my swollen and lifeless tongue can no longer speak, remember that I called upon Thee now.

Jesus, Mary, Joseph, to you I commend my soul.

## Favorite Holy Face Prayers

*(Added by the Publisher, 2010. From a leaflet published With Ecclesiastical Approval.)*

B E MERCIFUL to us, O my God, and reject not our prayers when, amid our afflictions, we call upon Thy Holy Name and seek with love and confidence Thine Adorable Face. Amen.

O ALMIGHTY and Eternal God, look upon the Face of Thy Son Jesus. We present It to Thee with confidence, to implore Thy pardon. The All-Merciful Advocate opens His mouth to plead our cause; hearken to His cries, behold His tears, O God, and through His infinite merits hearken to Him when He intercedes for us poor miserable sinners. Amen.

A DORABLE Face of my Jesus, my only Love, my Light and my Life, grant that I may know, love and serve Thee alone, that I may live with Thee, of Thee, by Thee and for Thee. Amen.

O DIVINE Jesus, through Thy Face and Name, save us. Our hope is in the virtue of Thy Holy Name!

ETERNAL Father, I offer Thee the Adorable Face of Thy Beloved Son for the honor and glory of Thy Name, for the conversion of sinners and for the salvation of the dying.